Knitting Makes You Fat

Every Blessing

L- Spriggs :-)

Poems & Yarns!

by

Alison Spriggs

First Edition

Printed by
FOR THE RIGHT REASONS
60 Grant Street, Inverness, IV3 8BS
Tel: 01463 718844 or 07717457247
Email: fortherightreasons@rocketmail.com
www.fortherightreasons.net

Acknowledgements

A BIG THANK YOU to:

Richard, Kev and all the volunteers at "For The Right Reasons" for all your dedicated hard work in publishing this book!

To Andy, for your help designing the cover.

To my friends in Sunset Café, keep up the good work, you are such an inspiration!

To all those who encouraged me and believed in me.

To my beloved husband, Steve and darling daughter, Rachel, my treasure and joy!

"To Him who loves us, be all the glory"

Alison

CONTENTS:

AGE

Oh to be older, when you're in your teens

The years ahead, so far it seems

Yet the older you get, the swifter they go

And you're nearing the end before you know.

A STRANGE OBSERVATION

Do you notice at this time when things are meant to be slicker

With the advancement in medicine, the people are sicker!

And in this time of great recession,

The ones with wealth, control and possession

Are the ones as far as I am seeing

That are meant to be looking after our well being!

AVOIDANCE

My clothes are tight and I'm getting fat,

But I don't want to talk about that.

I keep forgetting names, keys and to feed the cat

But I don't want to talk about that.

I've hit my forties, I'm getting on, it's a fact,

But I don't want to talk about that.

I didn't study hard, failed exams that I sat,

But I don't want to talk about that.

I hit the post, when reversing to park,

But I don't want to talk about that.

I'm spending too much money, that's a fact,

But I don't want to talk about that.

Burnt the dinner for guests, felt such a prat,

But I don't want to talk about that.

Dropped a tray of dishes as I slid on the mat,

But I don't want to talk about that.

A disaster with my hair lies under my hat,

But I don't want to talk about that.

Death, Eternity, Heaven and Hell is a fact,

But we don't want to talk about that.

BANK ACCOUNTS

It's so hard now to open a bank account,

When you want to deposit your little amount.

Forms to fill, references, two types of I.D

All to pay in your sum of money!

It's a difficult process, such a stress!

No wonder the banks are in such a mess!

The banks for your custom used to compete,

Delighted to see you, gave you a seat!

You just signed up and they did thank

Gave you a voucher and a piggy bank!

What if you won the lottery,

Had no account and no I.D?

BEAUTY ADVICE FOR WOMEN

Woman's sanity, I can't help but doubt,

When they go to the salon to get their eyebrows plucked out,

Why they go to all that expense and pain

Only to pencil them back in again?

I've never seen admiring glances from guys,

Wolf whistling at the sight of freshly plucked eyes!

So take my advice and save your money

There's better ways of looking yummy!

Though your hair is light and fair, going about town,

Your face and body's various shades of brown!

All sprayed on, your tan is fake!

Going about like a walking chocolate cake!

You've got plastic surgery on your face.

Your expression always stays in place!

Under the knife, or out of a can

You seem to think it'll get you a man!

BENEATH THE VEIL

Her eyes brimmed with tears, strained and pale

Hidden away, behind her veil.

Her true expressions you'll never see

Never gaze upon her real me.

Who is this stranger she's forced to marry?

Forever this burden she has to carry.

This veil covers her lips, she has no voice.

It covers her head, she has no choice!

Her life trapped in her black material den

Controlled from beginning to end by men

Walking behind them, ostracised

With no one to hear her silent cries.

BOXES

We enter this world, are placed in a clear plastic box and leave this world in a wooden box.

People who have lost the security of their home seek refuge in a cardboard box.

We go through our whole life, ticking and crossing boxes, boxes we are proud to be in and others we are not so happy about!

A box doesn't let you sit on the fence or change your mind, it restricts you and imprisons you!

A cross must be put in a box to vote for the leaders of our local area or nation and once our choice is made, we fold our paper and place it in yet another box!

Even God Himself, the Creator of the universe, we try to put in a box and keep the lid firmly shut! Not realising that if we opened it, the glorious, endless possibilities, beyond our limited imaginations are in that great adventure, if only we'd allow it to begin!

In His Kingdom, there are no boxes!

His gifts, no box can contain!

His cross, no one can put in a box!

BROKEN BOY

Robbed of childhood, tortured and scarred

Humiliated, abused, hurt and marred.

Emotions locked up in a den of fear

These eyes have never shed a tear.

To him no love is ever shown

Withdrawn and always on his own.

Drags his feet, eyes are down

On his face he wears a frown.

Though he walks past you and me

This horrific side we never see.

A well of emotions builds up inside

In no one he can confide.

There's none he trusts, hope is lost,

His heart is hard and cold, like frost.

From this life he tries to flee

But there's one who him can see.

Darkness surrounds him like the night

But He comes with a ray of light

In a church a song he hears

That dam it bursts, those eyes cry tears!

Something of the Saviour's care

Touches his life, so unfair.

His heart now like a broken shell

Emotions ruptured he starts to yell!

He now can see that God is there

Even through all this nightmare.

He takes a breath, it takes a while

His face breaks out into a smile!

CAPPUCCINO

The deafening aggressive rattle of the coffee grinder, as it pulverises these small, innocent, oily, dark brown, aromatic semi circular beans, showing them no mercy as it crushes them into fine rich powdery flakes.

Next into the press for their next stage of sadistic torture, where they are pushed down, flattened completely by a heavy metal vice, turned twice for two strong shots and drenched in scalding hot water, the dark smooth liquid espresso trickles out, caught by the tiny delicate espresso cup.

These beans reach their final destination, far travelled from the hot plantation of their Brazilian birth place.

As it is slowly dropping into the miniature cup, drip by drip, its rich aroma is tantalising my taste buds.

Milk from a local dairy in the seaside town of Nairn is poured into a shiny silver jug and placed under the curved, protruding, steel pipe. The dial above is turned clockwise, producing a hissing noise like an old steam engine, energising the milk into a crazy frenzy of tiny bubbles increasing this white liquid and changing its chemical composition, dramatically doubling it in size in seconds!

It is poured out carefully into the large, thick, royal blue Denby pottery cup, restraining the thick, white mallow foam back with a metal spoon, reserving it for later.

The treacly Brazilian liquid is poured into the milk, shading it with caramel coloured swirls and the pure, snowy, foam residue is spooned out on top, filling the cup to its brim.

It's carefully placed on matching saucer, with a teaspoon adorning its side.

A coffee bean template is placed over the steamy, hot drink and chocolate powder is gently dusted over depicting the humble bean in its original personified state as it proudly crowns my drink reminding me of the intense sacrifice it suffered in order to satisfy my caffeine craving.

As I sip the smooth, hot velvety liquid through the thick layer of frothy foam, its sense of humour still very much alive, as it dresses me with a moustache!

CHILD OF PROMISE

Awaited throughout history

To fulfil the ancient prophecy.

The virgin, conceived a child

All so pure and undefiled.

In a stable all forlorn

The child of promise, He was born!

The angels came, to shepherds sang,

To let them know His life began.

And there in a stable, in a manger bed,

Was the Child of promise, like the angels said!

Through a special star in the skies

The wise men learned of this surprise.

They told King Herod, they did choose

To worship this baby, King of the Jews.

Herod tried to have this baby killed

So this promise couldn't be fulfilled!

But God thwarted his evil plan

And the Child of promise became a man.

In wisdom and stature, this Child grew

Was loved by God and all He knew!

He healed the sick, restored the blind

He taught with wisdom and was kind.

He cast out demons, raised the dead,

Fed thousands with some fish and bread!

But the religious leaders they did cry,

This Child of promise, He must die!

He was betrayed by a friend

Crucified, His life would end.

He breathed his last, the veil was torn,

The end of the Child of promise born?

But just like He said and scripture says,

He rose again in three days!

So this Christmas as gifts we bring

And of this child of promise sing

Will you receive His gift so true?

This Child of promise is for you!

CHRISTMAS DAY

The turkey comes out, with every trimming

On to the table with food that's brimming!

I rescue my sausages in a bacon wrap

I must stay calm, not get in a flap!

At the door arrives my dear old aunt

In her hands a great big poinsettia plant!

Get out the crackers and the cranberry,

Oh and get the guests a sherry!

In spite of being filled to the top

Our Christmas pud, we eat the lot!

"Telly on!" My Aunt does screech!

"Quick, we're missing the Queen's speech!"

Sitting down to our coffee

Passing round the Thornton's toffee!

Can't manage cake or mince pie,

I'll be sick if I try!

Then after coffee, there's the game

Charades each year, it's the same!

Even with the same clues

Auntie still forgets the rules!

Then we'll open all the gifts

And organise the guests with lifts!

On reflection, next year we feel

We'll come to yours for our Christmas meal!

CONFESSIONS OF A BARGAIN HUNTER

I walk past the shop, stop,

See the sign "SALE"

Get excited

As I head straight for the bargain rail

I rummage through,

It's no surprise

There's nothing nice that's in my size!

Then an outfit catches my eye

That is so nice

Of course, I have to pay full price!

No returns and I can't try on

This sale really is a con.

All is not lost,

I see shoes in the sale

To go with my outfit

So blue and pale

I try to squeeze my feet

In shoes too small

And wobble in heels

That are far too tall!

Those that match

Are comfortable and nice,

You've guessed it

They're not half price!

My phone goes,

My friend shouts at me

The Co-op's got chickens down to 50p!

Down to the Co-op, fast as I can run

Out of breath, told,

Sorry she got the last one!

With their baskets brimming with chickens

All queued in front of me

As I make do with their offspring

And have their eggs for my tea

Mum says,

"It's not a bargain unless you need it"

Now that's a piece of advice

I should have heeded!

CUPCAKES

They're superior by far to any other bake,

Stealing the limelight, the proud cupcake!

Housed in a frilly, pretty delicate case,

Shop windows, weddings, all over the place!

They're used to celebrate every occasion,

The cupcake's getting above its station!

They've gone all designer, now so posh!

And they cost us lots of dosh!

No longer the common cupcake, forlorn.

The magazine covers, they now adorn!

Proudly displayed in their cake stands,

Baked all day, to meet demands!

People now make a career and trade,

Off the cupcakes they have made!

The other cakes didn't see this silent invasion,

The rising to fame of the cupcake creation!

In shock and horror, the chocolate éclairs,

In disbelief, just simply stares!

So envious is the custard slice,

Didn't treat the cupcake very nice!

Said the meringue, filled with cream,

"That cupcake has stole my dream!"

The right honourable Victoria sponge,

Will follow suit and take the plunge!

The yellow and pink squared battenburg,

Remained however, unperturbed!

"Listen up, our future's at stake,"

Said a very concerned Eccles cake!

People spot the cupcake when shopping,

Mouth watering at its lovely topping!

With its pretty, coloured sprinkles,

The cupcake just simply twinkles!

Crowned with a piece of fruit,

Who can resist? It looks too cute!

With no concern for another cake,

Straight for the cupcake people make!

The evidence of tell tale traces,

Icing smears on people's faces!

Very pleased is the popular cupcake,

At this great impression it has made!

DELL BOY

You're a Jack of all trades but master of none,

Living life in the fast lane, pretending it's fun!

In on the action, you're always there,

In the midst of trouble, but you don't seem to care!

Ducking and diving, trying to make money,

Conning the innocent, you think it's funny!

Even when caught, you slip like an eel,

You can't see how we hurt, don't care how we feel.

Your past catches up, from ones that did lend,

Didn't get you, it was your best friend.

In a hospital bed, fighting for his life,

With blows to his head and wounds from a knife!

Reality sinks in, your heart it does race,

As your friend like a brother, lies there in your place!

You pray through your tears, "God, his life don't take,

Please let him live, to mend my mistake."

Heaven hears your prayer, he opens his eyes

And the change in your life is a total surprise!

No longer on the run, no police at the door,

Our stuff is safe, you're not trying to score!

Your friend's on the mend, you've changed so much!

Now you're kind to all since you've gone to church!

Who would have thought, who could tell,

That this nightmare has saved you from Hell!

DISASTEROUS DATE

He went to meet her on their first date

Took a shortcut, as he was running late.

Cut through the woods and then got lost

And worst of all was stung by a wasp!

This was serious don't laugh or mock,

 Allergic, went into anaphylactic shock!

So Romeo there in the woods he did lie

If he wasn't found, he could die!

Thought she'd been stood up when 3 turned to 4

She ran out the house, slamming the door!

Ranting and raging and in a right stew,

Went down to the pub and had a few!

Then her nurse pal Sue, just off shift

Said something that gave her a lift,

"Oh yes, it was him I did see,

Rushed in on a trolley to A and E!"

Don't assume the worst, when he is late

Is the simple moral of this first date!

As he may be in a terrible plight

In the hospital with an insect bite!

EXPRESS YOURSELF

What I like about poems, is there are no rules
 You can write about anything you choose.
It doesn't matter if it rhymes or not
Your poem can be long or it can be short.
You get out anything you want to say
Any feelings or observations of the day
Emptying your head out on paper
For others to make sense of later!
Let your imaginations run totally free
Expressing the real inner me
It's really quite liberating
Satisfying that you are creating
Not bound by culture, sex or age
Past, present, futures on the page.
You don't need training or qualification
Just some encouragement and inspiration.
So what's in your head that needs to come out?
What do you want to tell others about?
So with you carry your pen and paper
And we look forward to hearing you later!

FAMILY WEDDING

You can tell when round the bend we're heading

We're getting ready for a family wedding!

Hotels and churches are gone around

Till the right ones can be found.

Bridesmaids to pick and best man

Present list to choose and plan.

Booking the minister and the church

Registering banns, so not left in the lurch!

Lists to be made of who to invite

Arguing who's coming, trying not to fight!

Plans for dresses, shoes and table seating,

The cake, the favours and what we're eating!

Invitations, name places to choose and to write

Vows to make, to learn and recite.

Trying on many dresses, altering to fit

Back again to the seamstress, my teeth I do grit!

What flowers to go for, fresh or dry?

Men in kilts or suit and tie?

Off to the jewellers to choose the ring

Order of service and songs to sing.

Choosing the photographer, viewing their pics

Accommodating guests thrown into the mix!

Hen and stag nights to arrange

Ideas for them a little strange!

Then who is filming this great event?

If anything left with the money that's spent!

Hairdressers booked, trials and appointments

Joys and thrills with some disappointments!

Shouts of, "hair comb, fascinator or hat?"

"Is this dress okay, does it make me look fat?"

Brochures out, planning a honeymoon

We'll all need a holiday pretty soon!

Then one of the guests who was going to sing

Turned up flashing her engagement ring!

She wondered why she got an upward stare

When she asked, "You wanna go to a wedding fare?"

FEELINGS LIKE SANDCASTLES

It seems so long since you said, "I do"

Sure it was for life, as you stood by the pew

Before God the Father and Jesus the Son

Something unique when you two became one.

Over the years, there's been a slow rift

On the tide of life, you've let your love drift.

But feelings like sandcastles are flimsy things

You need something more solid or they will grow wings.

Remember these dreams God placed in your heart?

Don't let the devil tear them apart.

Tides of life against you, You'll have many more

Opportunities for treasures in Heaven to store.

Lady Wisdom's your friend, I pray her you will find

Don't let these feelings ruin your mind.

So will you stick by him, through thick and through thin?

Or will you be like a sandcastle when the tide comes in?

FIRST DATE

My first date in style at the Wimpy we dined

Slidy, plastic red seats, but I didn't mind

Was all for the love of the knickerbocker glory!

No second date, that's the end of the story!

FREEDOM

Wake up broke and your head is sore,
Next weekend and you're back for more
If you have to cheat, if you have to steal,
Like a hamster, you're back on that wheel.
This is not the way it has to be,
He's calling you back to reality.

All you live for now is the end of the week,
The booze and the guys are the pleasures you seek,
Behind the make up, you can't disguise,
Hope is lost, there is pain in your eyes.
This is not the way it has to be,
He's calling you back to reality

Boys treat you bad and things turn sour,
The drink takes hold, you allow it power,
I feel sad when I see you go by,
We offer hope, wouldn't you give it a try?
This is not the way it has to be,
He's calling you back to reality.

GREAT GRACE

I cried out to you when I was lost,

You answered me and showed me the cross,

When I stop and look back,

I don't like what I see,

but when I stop and look up

you're smiling at me

And as my eyes of shame met your gaze,

you extended to me your great grace.

My past you choose no longer to see,

your eyes filled with love are always on me,

Despite what I've done, although I've run wild,

you've chosen me and called me your child.

Nothing in this world can ever replace

the restoration I've found through your great grace.

When I think of what you suffered to set me free,

it blows my mind what you've done for me,

To the nations the good news I'll tell,

this is the race I want to end well.

I choose to honour you and give you first place,

I'm so overwhelmed by your great grace.

GYM HEALTH WARNING

No, I tell you,
I'm not going to the gym!
No. No matter what state my body's in!
It's dangerous
To become a gym member!
Why?
Well, because of what happened last November.
It started when my friend joined, you see
And she got to take a friend for free
You guessed it, that friend was me!

I looked out my trainers and my track suit,
To be extra healthy, took a piece of fruit!
This was one of those posh ones, in a hotel
With a pool and a strong chlorine smell!
So, first we went on the big treadmill,
Which swallowed you up if you stood still!

Next, on to the safer option of a bike,
Where it was set for an uphill hike!
The seat was so hard and needed more padding
I felt sorry for those who had no cladding!
Fed up with the gym, we made for the pool,
Floundering at the side, feeling a fool.
We go to the shower, then when we come out
The fire alarm goes off and a great fuss is about!
Staff burst in, give a panicked shout,
It's a real fire and we have to get out!
Putting clothes on wet is hard, quite frankly,
When the towel given is the size of a hanky!

It's chaos, we're rushed
Informed of the dangers
I can't be seen like this by strangers!
To assemble in a car park
like this in November
Embarrassed
I just don't want to remember!
Insisting I'd rather burn than venture outside,
I was forced, stripped of clothes, dignity and pride!
It seemed to take the firemen so long to show
Then worst of all it started to snow!
Shivering cold, going blue
And turning to ice
For free exercise, now paying a great price!
It took so long till they let us back in
We lost the weight shivering ourselves thin!
So if a friend you want to the gym to go,
Don't ask me, cause I'll say, "NO"!!!!

HOME SWEET HOME

My home is a busy town on the coast

Some are incomers, but locals most

On the buses our Ma's a clippie

While Dad, he works at the local chippy!

Sisters and brothers, of each I have three

We live in a terrace house by the sea.

We have a dog and three cats, all are strays

And in the garden a hen that lays!

Out in the street, we love to play footy

Clothes passed down and looks from the snooty

Plenty of porridge and thick chunky bread

Seven hungry bairns have to be fed!

At seven exactly the steamer does dock

To the distant chimes of the old church clock

In our beds we're topped and tailed

"Off to sleep!" Our Mother wailed!

It's always noisy at number forty two

The kettle's on, come in for a brew!

HOMELESS

I wake up, though I never really sleep,
anyone could come,
thought they couldn't hurt me
anymore than I've been hurt.
I can't feel my hands and feet,
it's so cold! I hate this time of year,
I wish I had someplace to go,
just for today.

My chest is so sore when I cough,
I have cramps in my stomach,
but nothing can mask
the pain I feel inside!
I pull out my crumpled photos,
This is all I have left in the world.
I look at my Mum's pretty face,
She was so happy then,
Why did she have to die?

Sometimes when I shut my eyes
All I hear is the screaming,
The screaming is me.
I cover my ears,
I hear the voices taunting me,
telling me I'm good for nothing,
I don't want to listen,
not today!

I often think of sweet little Jodie
with her lovely big eyes,

pleading with me to take her to the park,
I'll never forget the day they took her into care,
That was the last I saw of my sister,
But I mustn't get upset, no, not today!

Where will I go today?
I think I'd like to go to the museum,
I'd get a bit of warmth.
Then I remember the last time I was there
and was thrown out,
everyone staring at me,
No, I wouldn't put myself
through that humiliation,
not today!

I wander down town,
I sit in my favourite doorway,
anyone who as much as glances at me,
looks away quickly and hurries on.
I suppose I can't blame them,
A few years ago I'd have done the same!
Let's face it,
I'm not exactly a pretty sight,
These clothes are all I've got,
Goodness knows how long
I've had them on for!
Still, if you're dirty and smelly,
It keeps people from getting too close!
I look at the girl walking past with the Big Mac,
I hate being reminded of how hungry I am!
If only I could have one, just for today!

I see a lad, not much younger than me,
Shouting at his Mum,
demanding money for some computer game.
It makes me so mad!
I feel like punching his lights out!
He doesn't know how lucky he is
to have his Mum around!
I wish my Mum was here,
I miss her so much!
I hear people talking about me,
I feel like shouting,
I may be dirty, but I'm not deaf,
Instead I just hang my head in shame.
It's after lunch time,
I wander up towards the shopping centre,
yes, the seagulls are hovering,
that looks promising!
I put my hand in the bin
And find a few chips in their container.
I used to worry about people seeing me,
Now I don't care! A bit cold,
But the best I've eaten in a while.
I take a wander down to the public toilets,

The tap water there was not the best to drink,
but it will do.
I throw some water over my face,
Gosh, I do look a sight!
It's getting colder!

I hate this time of year!
Maybe I'll do something,

just to get a night in the cells,
a clean bed, a hot cup of tea,
a decent meal,
a nice hot shower,
it sounds good!
I mull it over,
perhaps, seeing as it's today!

Walking along,
I see an empty beer bottle on the wall,
no, wait a minute, there's a little left at the bottom.
I hold it up to my dry cracked lips,
drain the dregs and wish myself a Happy Birthday!

HOPE IN PAIN

I know things you've been through have been really bad

And it breaks my heart to see you so sad

Don't just give up, fight through the pain

There's always a rainbow after the rain.

Take time to heal, give life a chance,

There's a time to mourn and a time to dance.

Your tears they have flowed and heartache you've seen

On the other side the grass will be green.

So look up to the One where your help comes from

He can heal the pain of all that's gone wrong.

So take heart, hold on and don't let go

Don't always say yes, learn to say no!

He'll wipe away every tear from your eye

A hope for you future ahead it doth lie.

HORRENDOUS HAIR DO

In my face my hair does go

Grey's appearing, roots do show

To the hairdressers, time I went

In I go for my appointment

Colour charts, with each shade

With a lock of hair all displayed

From very dark, to very light

Or vibrant reds and colours bright

She brushes on the colour mixed

Looks nothing like the one I picked!

The chemicals in the colour dye

Stings my eyes and makes me cry!

Head full of silver squares, what fun

And down my face mascara's run

In the mirror I'm a horrific vision

For Dr Who I could audition!

I'm such a sight, I can't be seen

I hide behind my magazine

In the chair, with head in foils

Forced to listen to Chris Moyles!

Busy chatting about her holiday

While she's chopping all my hair away

My lovely locks, all on the floor

Not content, she cuts some more!

To my appearance, she's making corrections

While pulling my hair in all directions!

When rinsing, she my head does scald

Not much left, I'm nearly bald!

On goes the dryer, burning my head

Now I can't hear a word she's said!

Hairspray? I say, "Yes please."

She sprays a lot, I start to sneeze!

She holds up a mirror, I view the back

Oh my goodness, what a lot she did hack!

Then sixty quid from me she did rip,

Well I hope she wasn't expecting a tip!

HOUSE HUNTING

I'm off to view a house today

Making observations on my way.

The street is long and it does wind

Will my house be hard to find?

House on one side, curtains drawn

Grass high, don't mow their lawn.

The house itself is fairly plain

The rest in the street just the same.

Garden with wildflowers takes pride

I glance next door to the other side,

Bobbing heads above the hedge are seen

The kids must have a trampoline.

The shops and schools aren't too far

But there's not a drive to park the car.

The hinge is broken on the gate

The roof is missing at least one slate!

Up from the path sprouts a few weeds

A small mucky pond full of reeds.

I step up to the door, am ushered in

Tour the lounge, diner and the kitchen.

Seventies décor all around

Hardly a cupboard to be found!

Up we go, the stairs that creak

Hear a drop, "Oh, that's the leak!"

Bedrooms, with sheets of flannelette

Dressing table with vanity set!

In the bathroom a knitted doll guards the roll

Carpet on the seat and round the pedestal!

In the garden I spot a long washing line!

"Yes, I'll take it, when can we sign?"

I MISS WOOLIES! - By Alison Spriggs

Going to Woolie's was one of my favourite treats

Where I immediately headed straight for the sweets!

So much to choose from, so much to eat

Sugared almonds, nougat and Quality Street.

What will I choose, where will I start?

Milk bottles, bon-bons or a love heart?

Marshmallows, pear drops, coconut ice,

Any of these would be very nice!

Chocolate peanuts, raisins and Turkish delight

My mouth was watering at the sight

Sherbet lemons, fudge and soor plums

Gobstoppers, Murray mints and fruit gums.

Treacle toffee, pandrops and cola cubes,

Humbugs, puff candy, or dube dubes?

Refreshers, bubble gum or a banana foam,

Just what sweets will I take home?

Strawberry laces, odd fellows and clove rock

Jelly babies, black jacks and a chocolate drop

Barley sugars, boilings and chocolate éclairs,

Liquorice allsorts, white mice and gummy bears!

Lucky tatties, chewits and aniseed balls,

I try to hide when my mother calls!

"That's enough now, you'll be sick"

Just a jelly snake and a drumstick?

As I take it carefully up to the till,

I eat a few, so I don't spill!

Then I'd go home and eat all this

Woolies pick a mix I miss!

I'M FINE

Was to meet him at 8, it's now after 9

No, I'm not worried, I'm really fine!

Didn't exit the motorway, missed the sign

Lost and late, but I'm really fine!

Kids not happy, they just seem to whine

Getting on my nerves, but I'm really fine!

Got food poisoning, when out we did dine

I'll stay by the toilet, but I'm really fine!

The fish was so big, it got off my line

I'm so disappointed, but I'm really fine!

Someone left their luggage and took mine

Just got what I'm wearing, but I'm really fine!

Was asked how I was when I had bad flu

Being me said fine, but that wasn't true!

But this is the case half of the time

When I smile and answer, " I'm really fine!"

IN DEFENCE OF BRUSSELS SPROUTS

Of the humble Brussels sprout

There's really not much said about

Out at Christmas to dress the bird

Aside from that, not a word!

As a vegetable, not a popular dish

It definitely can't be served with fish!

So this Christmas, let's spare it a thought

It's the only time it seems to be bought!

Then a surprise, to break the ice

One sold on Ebay at a great price!

The closet sprout lover came out

To salvage the reputation of the Brussels sprout!

Like mini cabbages, they're almost cute

Neatly dressed in a lovely green suit,

They may get a complex, so don't them hate

Or leave them lying at the side of your plate!

INSPIRATION

Looking through the pages of history

Full of men and women we aspire to be.

One stands out above them all

A rescue plan He formed when man did fall.

He paid the price we couldn't afford.

I want to be like You, My Lord.

JACK FROST

When temperatures drop, he will appear,

Jack Frost, to chill the atmosphere!

Jack Frost, with his icy bite,

Turns cobwebs into silver white!

Bin lids, car doors, he spreads thick,

His Jack Frost glue, to make them stick!

And for a laugh, just for a joke,

Jack Frost makes us breathe out smoke!

KNITTING MAKES YOU FAT

It all started when Mother got needles and wool,

And patterns for jackets that weren't very cool

It seemed to catch on as my grannies did too

Making jackets of pink, white, yellow and blue.

Mary came each week, with her needles and wool

I may just be three, but I am no fool

She'd come for tea and they'd chat a bit

But most of the time they'd sit and knit!

A strange thing happened, I tell you it's true

The more things they knitted, their tummies they grew!

As time went by, they got in such a state

All this knitting made them so overweight!

Then once when asleep, on went the light

I was put to granny's, in the night!

Taken to the hospital, the very next day

Where there in a bed, my mother did lay

I ran up to her and said that I missed her

And she replied, "Say hello to your sister!"

I turned round and there in a small clear box

Lay a little doll with soft brown locks.

Then her face crumpled up, she began to cry

Mum was taking her home, I didn't know why?

Though I have to put up with the noise and the din

The knitting is over and Mum's getting thin!

LETTER TO SANTA

Dear Santa,

If you're as good as you seem

How come bad kids

Get all the good toys?

These brats that are really rude

That scream, demand

And make a noise?

I really think Santa

It's time to up your game

And treat kids with equality

Fair and square

Insuring that the good kids

Get the best or

At the very least

Their fair share!

Now Santa,

You really shouldn't

Discriminate

In this day and age

Be more P.C

As most houses are centrally heated

And for you

They don't have a chimney!

I think Santa

A bad example you set

Into one night

All your work you do cram

And worst of all,

Kids you encourage

To give a mince pie

And pour you a dram!

Well Santa,

I hope you have a disclosure

As child protection

Would find it quite shocking

Entering all these children's bedrooms

With the excuse of filling their stocking!

And Santa,

In this time of recession

In this day and age

When funds are low

Where do you get the money

For all these toys?

And tell me,

Does the Tax man know?

Now Santa,

Please search your conscience

You and Mrs Claus

Need to ask yourselves

Are you adhering to employment law?

Or are you exploiting these elves?

Now Santa,

I do hope your passport is valid

Just because your name is Santa Claus

Travelling round the world

From Lapland

You have to abide

By the immigration laws!

Now Santa,

You're mistreating your reindeer

I have to report you

To the R.S.P.C.A

These poor beasts

Carry an overweight you

All these toys

And your great big sleigh!

Now Santa,

I'm shocked in this season

With drinking all these drams

On the way

To the police

I should really report you

With drinking,

While driving a sleigh!

Now Santa,

Regarding these matters

And I'm sure there's many I've missed

In the season of goodwill

I'll turn a blind eye

If you bring

All I've enclosed on my list!

LIONS

Driving through the Safari Park, into the lion enclosure.

These great beasts, the kings of the jungle, lie motionless, unperturbed by our arrival.

They laze around, basking in the morning sunshine.

We are stopped right beside them, so close I could almost touch that beautiful mane, if I dared to reach out!

They look so docile and placid, even deceivingly friendly.

I wonder what would happen if I opened the door and got out to stroke this awesome beauty of a beast?

I am tempted like Eve with the fruit, but with the knowledge that the ramifications of my choice would have the same result - Death!

LOOKING FOR LOVE

Looking for love in the wrong place

Lonely and sad 'neath a made up face.

That happy ever after to make everything right

You're hoping to find this very night.

You spend all that time just doing your hair

Trying not to think, like you just don't care

The real you cased in a thick hard shell

As you try and pretend that all is well

As he comes towards you across the dance floor

He's used that chat up line many times before

Beneath his smile, it's all a lie

He'll have his way and make you cry.

Say, "No", get up, walk out the door

You see, you are worth so much more

Just come to the one who understands

Your name is written on His nail pierced hands.

MASSACRE

To a school on your path of destruction did go,

With evil intent, no mercy did show.

Gunning down lives

of those you didn't know!

Shooting children, teachers and even the head,

No thought for their lives, just killed them all dead

Our hearts they did ache, as the TV did show,

Innocent faces of kids we didn't know!

Though Obama will visit, what hope can he bring?

To the families bereft of their most precious thing.

So this Christmas, make sure a prayer is said

For the unfortunate ones who bury their dead!

Nearer to home, of something the same,

It reminds us of those lost in Dunblane.

The world is behind you, as we share in your sorrow

May the Lord give you His comfort and hope for tomorrow!

MEN AND WOMEN

Us women
Have wardrobes jammed packed full
But we still have nothing to wear
While you men
Seem to wear the same thing
And quite frankly
You don't care!

Us women
When getting ready to go out
It takes us time
And effort to prepare
While you men
On a special occasion
May take a comb
Through your hair!

Us women,
Chocolate is our weakness
What angers us by far
Is the new packaging wrap
'Men only'
On the Yorkie bar!

Us women

When it comes to cars

Pick something reliable

That will last

While you men

 On the other hand

Love cars

That are flashy and fast!

Us women

Like our soppy novels

Where in love they fall

While you men

Let your emotions show

Watching

A game of football!

Us women

Enjoy mouth watering delicacies

To pass between our lips

While you men

On the other hand

Would rather pie and chips!

Us women

Have a different bag

To match our many shoes

And every time we buy another

You men

You blow a fuse!

Us women

Love our sparkly bling

You men are all the same

You love the latest gadget

Or playing

A computer game!

Us women

With a problem

At once

For help will shout

You proud men

On the other hand

Try for days, in vain

To figure it out!

Us women's

favourite past time

Is a good chat

Or a shopping spree

While you men are quite content

To sit at home

And watch T.V!

MISSING CHILD

Out in the garden, one sunny day
On the rug, with my daughter at play.
I ran into the house, to get her a hat
I wasn't a minute, if even that.

When I came back the truth it did dawn
I couldn't see her, my daughter had gone!
My heart beat faster, I got in a state
When I noticed unlocked was the gate!

I ran out of the garden, on to the street
Shouted at neighbours and all I did meet!
Looked everywhere, but she couldn't be found
In the distance the sirens sound.

Police came in, questions did ask
As a mother I felt I'd failed at my task!
Of what she was wearing, a description they took
And wrote it all down in their little note book.

I tried to answer, sobbing and shaking
From this nightmare, I wish I was waking!

People wanted to help and over they came

Police asked for a picture, I had one in a frame.

I went through to get it, feeling the worst

So overwhelmed, I thought I would burst!

I went into her room and there on her bed

Lay my daughter asleep with her little Ted!

MISSING HOME

I am miserable, stuck in this high rise flat

In the centre of this busy, unfriendly, noisy city.

I am missing home, I feel so far away

And I feel a lump come to my throat.

My eyes catch sight

Of the large, beautiful shell on the shelf,

I pick it up and carefully examine it

Wondering what creature it housed

That so graciously gave up its home for me?

I hold it close up to my ear,

Close my eyes

And I listen to the sound of the sea,

I'm home.

MY FIRST CAR

So pleased with the purchase of my first car

That was short lived, I didn't get very far!

When just less than a mile from the garage

Something fell off my undercarriage!

I slowed right down, pulled into the side

Got out the car and hitched a ride

Back to the garage, was as cross as could be

As they said, "Not covered by the guarantee!"

To fix the problem, the money spent

Was all I had left to pay the rent

Skint and hungry and having to walk

This was the worst thing I'd ever bought!

MY LOVE FOR YOU

My love for you is a never ending chasm that I am continually falling deeper and deeper into.

NEIGH NIGHTMARE

My friend suggested a trek, such a glorious day,

"Sounds like fun," I heard myself say.

Having never rode, in ignorant bliss,

I arrived at the stables and there I met Chris.

She took one look at me, asked, "How much do you weigh?"

Horrified, I was embarrassed to say!

"By the look of you, you'll need the shire,"

The horse was massive, you couldn't get higher!

Well trying to get on it, Chris tried to teach,

"Put your foot in the stirrup," but mine wouldn't reach!

Every way she said, I tried each,

Oh, how I wished I'd suggested the beach!

She got my foot in the stirrup, I thought it would break!

"Grab the saddle, push up, for goodness sake!"

My legs didn't like being stretched that wide,

Then my trousers ripped inside!

With many attempts to push and pull,

They finally resorted to using a stool!

Half an hour later I was sat on top

Hat on head, in hand a crop.

"Take the reins in your hands, sit up straight,

Give a kick to the sides, go through the gate."

I felt a bit wobbly and held on real tight,

When the horse went faster, I got such a fright!

Then up through the forest, in a gentle stride,

I began to relax and enjoy the ride!

A thought filled me with fear, I could not discount,

How on earth was I going to dismount?

When at last it came to an end,

Mental note to self, my trousers must mend!

"Take your feet out the stirrups, swing your leg, slide down"

"I'm trying honest," I cried with a frown!

Trying as I might, I was truly stuck,

They laughed when I suggested a tractor and truck!

When I started to fear I was going to fall,

Chris led me beside the stable wall.

"Put your foot on it and give a big push"

Was a good plan, till the horse got loose!

With a foot in the stirrup and one on the wall,

I looked such a sight as I started to fall!

"Why does this have to happen to me?"

As I landed in muck, rubbing my knee!

One things for sure, all things aside,

Never again a horse will I ride!

OUR MASKS

I look into the mirror and staring at me
Is the face I put on for the world to see.
What's in my mind, hid by make up and skin
Would shock you to see the state it's in!
What's behind that mask to be set free,
Is the lost and broken real me.
It is a problem, quite a task,
To free a person from their mask.
What will help to lift this screen?
Encouragement raises self esteem
If with your words you criticise
This mask you will never prise.
We're all the same, like Stepford wives
Masks in place, to hide our lives.
So let us this situation improve
And one by one, our masks remove.
With our words, let's speak in kind,
Of our good points, us remind.
Always try and be positive
And with mistakes, please forgive.
For others, let's compassion feel
So masks come off and we are real!

PRESS ON

Lots of us have been so keen at the start

Most wandered off and lost heart.

Even though the rest are gone

You move forward and press on!

Like others, don't you compromise

You press on to win the prize

To finish well is the goal

Don't gain the world and lose your soul!

Take the opportunities, seize the day

Encourage others on the way

Go to the ones that He does send

To all the lonely, be a friend!

Don't get tired of doing good

Treat people like you know you should

Whatever obstacle you may face

You press on and run the race!

RODGER DODGER

Rodger, together, I thought we'd last,

Before you lied about your past.

Can't build a future, if you I don't trust,

You've really hurt me, you don't seem fussed!

Rodger, to you I can't seem to get through

You don't carry out what you say you will do.

You wouldn't ever think to apologise

To be considerate, or even compromise!

At me you were angry, at me you did shout

So it's over Rodger, over and out!

SEALS

After a hard days hunting, my belly is full of fish. The tide pulls back and I seek out my favourite rock, facing the road and I lie basking in the warm sunshine.

I look around and see my friends, perched on their adjacent rocks contentedly.

A car pulls up in the nearby lay-by and its passenger points a camera in my direction, I pose obligingly and he continues on his journey.

I count the passing cars until I fall into a peaceful slumber. Till the tide wakes me and takes me and it's time to go fishing again.

SUNSET CAFÉ

On Church Street, Sunset Café's the place,

Anita to greet you, with a smile on her face!

With warm décor of orange and brown,

The place to be seen, the talk of the town!

Coffees of every kind and description,

To caffeine lovers, the very prescription!

Speciality teas, of every flavour,

To enjoy to sip and to savour!

Chilled drinks, fruit juices and fresh milkshakes

And beautiful warming soup she makes!

Paninis, toasties, sandwiches and may I just say,

You can now have breakfast anytime of the day!

It's all there, for a very good price,

So polish it off with something nice!

The hot Belgium waffles are a recommendation!

With fruit, sauce and cream, a taste sensation!

Try some of Anita's new home bakes,

Chocolate, lemon drizzle or carrot cakes!

Anita, for you can cater outside,

With a fabulous buffet she will provide!

Plenty for you to taste and try,

Art to view and to buy!

And if poems, you do write

Come and share on a Saturday night!

Whether it's for an ice cream on a hot day,

Or a hot chocolate, to warm you on your way

Or sampling the coffee, the various blends

You'll leave with a smile, having made friends!

TALK TO HIM

When scared and desperate and can't find a way

 As a last resort, we might just pray?

Don't blame Him for actions others have done

To buy your freedom, it cost Him His Son.

He just wants to hear what you've got to say

So talk to Him now and you'll make His day!

TEARS IN HIS BOTTLE

Her tears in His bottle

He's gathered with care

Always before Him

He heard every prayer

There's beauty for ashes

She will dance and not mourn

With a life everlasting

Where death is no more

Like every believer

At last she can be

Forever with Jesus

Who now she can see

Her pain has all gone now

Crying no more

No hurt can be felt there

Beyond Heaven's door

She's rejoicing in Heaven

As she turns to Him

As Her precious Saviour

Welcomes her in

Hear the sound of my Father

As He sings over me

There in His presence

Where I want to be

Now your tears in His bottle

He's collecting with care

You're never alone now

My Jesus is there

TECHNO GENERATION

Where are our dreamers, where are their dreams?

Lost in their phones, behind computer screens.

'Neath cyber space lying, creativity dying.

Discoveries now learned from facebook,

I dare not get sucked in and look!

Where are the boys that climb the trees?

No cowboys and Indians, all that's ceased.

Where are the girls, with their skipping ropes?

Where are their dreams, where are their hopes?

Go to the shelf, pick up a book,

By pass google and take a look.

Loose your imaginations from this cage,

Don't be robbed in this technology age!

No footballs, bikes in sheds, streets silent,

Behind screens, playing games of violence.

We wonder how they turn out bad and mean?

When reality's behind a computer screen!

Communicating only by email and text

Is how they get by one day to the next.

No more written letters, the phone never rings,

Just their mobiles with texts they will ping!

Notepads electronic, iPod and iPad,

The techno invasion's getting quite bad!

Seems like everyone in each house,

Is controlled by the click, of one small mouse!

THE DECISION

What to do about you, I just don't know?

I got on a bus, not sure where to go?

I got on wondering what to do later

And sat next to a man, reading his paper.

A little girl in front, her hair in pleats,

Kept getting up and changing seats!

I smiled and thought, she's just like me,

Indecisive and all at sea!

I glance at his paper and there to my shame

The story is there and it's you they do blame!

You say it's all lies, it's simply not true,

You say you were framed, what do I do?

My heart beats loud, as I glance at your text,

You got bail, want to meet, so what next?

To meet you at our usual coffee shop,

Means getting off at the next stop!

To see you there inside at three

It seems too much, too fast for me!

The bus stops, I rise but just change seats,

Just like the little girl in pleats!

THE JOURNEY

This journey, though short,

Seems the longest I've been on.

Staring out of the police car window,

Everyone I pass is rushing about,

It's business as usual,

But for me

Life will never be the same again.

Time stands still,

As life has dealt me its cruellest blow.

The pain is so intense,

It has reached below the place of feelings

I am completely numb.

What I am about to do

No mother should have to face.

My mind's all in a blur and haze,

As the child I bore,

lies lifeless,

beyond that mortuary door.

THE PRODIGAL

There's nothing this world has to offer,

Money can't fill this void

How did I end up in this state?

Every hope and dream is destroyed.

I remember, there's a God in Heaven,

Have I strayed from beyond His grace?

My heart it begins to quicken,

As the tears run down my face.

My past, it comes up to haunt me,

All the guilt that I feel inside

But He sees me coming in the distance,

His arms are open wide!

He's running now towards me,

Going that extra mile,

His eyes look pleased to see me,

His face breaks into a smile

A ring and robes, are placed upon me,

As I fumble my apology

Not looked upon as a servant,

He welcomes me as royalty!

His forgiveness, it overwhelms me,

As I fall into His embrace

Sick and tired of all this running,

He kisses the tears from my face.

There's a place set at His table,

A place that's just for me

How His heart aches when it's empty,

How foolish can I be.

Another place is set at His table,

Where a welcome waits for you

My Father He's waiting in the distance,

Longing for you to come too.

THE SEAGULL HAS LANDED

If you happen to go down to the beach

Make sure you keep food out of reach

These greedy gulls your food will seek

Hover round with open beak

They are not fussy, they scavenge in bins

Looking for leftovers, in packets and tins.

At picnics they are the uninvited guests

To the birdfeeders, they are such pests!

An innocent child eating their piece

A seagull swoops, them he does fleece.

No conscience, motivated only by food

Don't wait to be offered they are very rude!

Like Hitchcock's birds, they're really bad

When folk feed them, it makes me mad!

They're so selfish, think it their right

To gobble up all that's in sight!

Like addicts, food they crave

Grabbing, stealing, they misbehave!

If you've just washed your car, beware

They'll splat right on it from the air!

They smell chips 100 miles away!

Roost in towns and cities, here to stay

The curse of these dirty, flying bandits

Look out now the seagull has landed!

THE SOUND OF SILENCE

Running, barking, braying, yelping sounds

A fox is chased, by all these hounds!

Silence now, foxes safe at protesters'f demands

As at last this cruel sport is banned!

THE TORTOISE'S SECRET

I don't worry about time,

Laze about, the day is mine!

Others rushing, to work they go,

Me, I take it nice and slow!

When the trees, their colours change

And pattern paths, with leaves arrange.

When the autumn's getting late,

I get tired and hibernate!

I miss the frights of Halloween,

Those ghosts and ghouls I've never seen!

I miss Guy Fawkes, the Christmas rush!

I'm sleeping, be quiet, now hush!

I miss the snow and all the ice,

The better weather's very nice!

My home's not used for entertaining,

I've always shelter when it's raining!

No one in my home with whom to fight,

Days and evenings, long and light!

The birds return, a song they sing,

To wake me up in time for spring!

It's because I have no stress or strife,

I live a long and happy life!

THOUGHTS OF PLAY

Remember back to, I'm scared to say

Of the toys and games we used to play

Racing scalextric and card tricks

Joining together our stickle bricks!

Constructing structures from meccano

Plonking a tune on my toy piano!

Roller skates to make you go

Pulling sledges through the snow!

Drawing with my etcha a sketch

Bendy dolls that you could stretch.

Adventures with Sindy or Action man

Excited by the sound of the ice cream van!

Simple games with a bat and ball

Pressing out a dress up doll!

Reading Beano, Beezer and The Dandy,

Twinkle, Jackie, Blue Jeans and Mandy!

Sand pits, bikes and skipping games,

Flying kites and model planes

Watching Starsky and Hutch and The A Team

While fizzing drinks in our soda stream!

Feeding and changing my tiny tears

Takes me back a good few years!

TYPIST REQUIRED

I started a job in a typing pool

The girls there were all so cruel!

Their stiletto heels and hair in a bun

Serious looks, they were no fun!

Whispered to each other, looking at me

I asked if they'd like coffee or tea?

My efforts to befriend, they seemed to ignore

Without saying goodbye, they'd go out the door.

I decided to keep a good attitude

In spite of the fact they were being so rude

I bought in fresh coffee and cakes

Always smiled, overlooked their mistakes.

Gossiping, swearing and all the backstabbing

No please or thank you, just pinching and grabbing!

Then with a book, over the head I was hit

I ran into the office and said that I quit!

WHAT'S YOUR CHOICE?

We are all different, we're all unique

From our looks, our opinions, the way we speak.

Yet in common, we're all born, we all die,

We all hurt, we all hide, we all laugh, we all cry.

On our journey of life, the routes that we take,

Are determined by the choices we make.

Do we hide behind a cloak of mystery?

Let our destiny be dictated by history?

This life we live, we only have one

Soon disappearing, like the setting of sun.

Before it's too late, before you depart,

Please take time to examine your heart.

Till the time of goodbyes and they all shed a tear,

Don't enter your box, till your exit is clear!

WHY

Why do caterpillars become butterflies?

Why a child our patience tries?

Why with others do we compare?

Why do women iron their hair?

Why is it hard to say goodbye?

Why do people have to die?

Why do some get allergies?

Why doesn't money grow on trees?

Why have zebras got those stripes?

Why do kilted men play pipes?

Why blow a candle with a wish?

Why betray the Lord with a kiss?

Why do Sat Navs confuse?

Why does Scotland always lose?

Why are snowflakes never the same?

Why do I forget your name?

Why do new shoes always hurt?

Why do children play in dirt?

Why after the jab, do we get flu?

Why when you need it is there no loo?

Why eat our eggs out a cup?

Why do families split up?

Why going to the dentist do we dread!

Why's my bank balance in the red?

Why do people hit the booze?

Why do gamblers always lose?

Why on a good day wear a hood?

Why choose bad, instead of good?

Why in queues do we have to wait?

Why's the country in such a state?

I guess the state of every nation

Can be traced back, to Creation.

WILD CHILD

About to indulge in a spot of retail therapy

When a young Mum and her child I do see.

"Mum, please can I have this magazine?"

"It's the best one I've ever seen!"

"No, you can't, not today,

Wait till Friday when I get my pay."

Not satisfied with this answer,

He lifted the comic, the little chancer!

His voice it rose three octaves high

"I WANT IT NOW" he did cry!

"No, I told you, now put it back!"

I thought, he's heading for a smack!

"But it's got a free game," he wailed

Mum's efforts calming him all failed!

He screamed and screamed and stamped his feet

This boy didn't deserve a treat!

If we did that, they'd call the police

Charge us with, a breach of the peace!

WINTER

It's getting dark, when it's still day

You can see that winter's on its way.

On a clear night, seeing the stars

We're scraping ice off our cars!

Chimneys, with smoke they puff

Mother's making clootie duff,

Christmas cakes and mince pies

No doubt we'll all go up a size!

Candles, carols and mulled wine

Nativity plays, the pantomime.

Christmas, its true meaning lost

Commercialized and killed by cost.

In the sales, for bargains there's riots

And the overindulged are all on diets!

WONDERS OF CREATION

The seasons follow each other like sheep, called forth by The Shepherd.

The waves of the sea dare only to go so far and then draw back reluctantly. They will sometimes however, get very brave, when they are angry and like us, they will push the boundaries!

The mountains stand faithfully, displaying their majesty through the ages, while others bored, with staying faithful, blow their top, literally!

YOUR BRIDEGROOM

At the party you mingle,

Trying to find out who's single,

While your Bridegroom awaits

At Heaven's Gates.

No matter who you choose,

In love you always seem to lose.

His love will take away your fear

To you, He longs to draw near.

While others are passing

His love is everlasting.

Wake up! Dust yourself down,

On your head He'll place a crown.

Don't delay or hesitate and wait

Run to Him before it's too late.

All the things of this world will rust

Our bodies will turn back to dust.

But you are precious in His sight,

He calls you out the dark, into the light.

For you, your Bridegroom awaits

His arms are open at Heaven's gates.

YOUR CHOICE

You chose me, before You even created this world. You decided exactly in the span of time, when I would be born, to the very second.

You decided what race, culture, period, parentage and family I would arrive into.

You longed for my arrival and watched over me as I was born, the proud Father!

You have also chosen the time and place of my departure from this world.

In between my arrival and departure, You take a step back, allowing me the freedom to make my own choices, forever hoping and longing for me, to choose You!